Top Dog

The Samoyed

by William R. Sanford and Carl R. Green

CRESTWOOD HOUSE

New York

CIP

LIBRARY OF CONGRESS CATALOGING IN PUBLICATION DATA

Sanford, William R. (William Reynolds)
  Samoyed

  (Top dog)
  Includes index.
  SUMMARY: Discusses the history, physical characteristics, care, and breeding of this medium-sized dog known for its ability to withstand the cold.
  1. Samoyeds (Dogs) — Juvenile literature. [1. Samoyeds (Dogs) 2. Dogs.] I. Green, Carl R. II. Title. III. Series: Sanford, William R. (William Reynolds), Top dog.
SF429.S35S26   1989   636.7'3 — dc20   89-31070
ISBN 0-89686-451-0

PHOTO CREDITS

Cover: Elfenbein Samoyeds: Jim & Elfie Shea
Elfenbein Samoyeds: (Jim & Elfie Shea) 4, 9, 14, 25, 27, 35, 38, 40
Animals Animals: (Roger & Donna Aitkenhead) 11
DRK Photo: (Stephen J. Krasemann) 20
Photo Researchers, Inc.: (Kent & Donna Dannen) 17, 28, 46

Macmillan Publishing Company
866 Third Avenue
New York, NY 10022
Collier Macmillan Canada, Inc.

CRESTWOOD HOUSE

Produced by Carnival Enterprises

Printed in the United States of America

First Edition

10 9 8 7 6 5 4 3 2 1

TABLE OF CONTENTS

FOR MORE INFORMATION

For more information about Samoyeds, write to:

American Kennel Club
51 Madison Avenue
New York, NY 10010

Samoyed Club of America
P.O. Box 185
Waldo, WI 53093

THE FIRST DOGS IN SPACE

Storm growled deep in his throat when the front door slammed. Clara Mulqueen held the eager Samoyed steady. "Easy, Storm," she said. "That will be Sheila, or I miss my guess. No one else enters our house like a runaway rocket."

A moment later, Sheila ran in to give her grandmother a hug. Then she turned to Storm. In a moment, girl and dog were wrestling on the floor. The play fight broke up when Storm's long tongue flicked out and licked Sheila's chin.

"Okay, I give up!" Sheila yelled. Then she picked up a brush and began *grooming* Storm's pure white fur. "Gram," the girl said at last, "today's the day you promised to clear up the mystery."

"What mystery, dear?" Clara said.

"You know," Sheila insisted. "I want to know why Storm's full name is Space Storm of Gresham. Gresham's the name of our town, but isn't Space Storm a strange name for a Samoyed?" She said *Sam-a-YED*, just as Clara had taught her.

People have been breeding and training Samoyeds for at least 3,000 years. That makes this dog one of the world's oldest breeds. 5

Clara settled into her rocking chair. "It's a strange story," she said. "It goes back to the late 1950s. Back then, the Russians were launching the first space satellites. When their second satellite went up, it had a dog aboard. Everyone called the dog Laika, which is Russian for any huskylike breed of dog."

"Did Laika live through the flight?" Sheila wondered.

"No," Clara said sadly. "The Russians didn't have any way to bring Laika back to Earth. That all changed when another satellite was launched in 1960 with two dogs on board."

"Why were they sending animals into space?" Sheila asked. "The dogs couldn't tell anyone what was happening."

"Ah, but they could," Clara told her. "Inside their space suits, the dogs were wired to monitors. The scientists on Earth could check things like pulse rate and blood pressure."

"I wouldn't let anyone do that to Storm!" Sheila protested.

Clara ruffled her granddaughter's hair. "The dogs were space pioneers," she said. "No one knew if living things could survive in outer space."

"Well, what happened?" Sheila demanded.

"After a day in space, the dogs' space capsule was parachuted back to Earth. When they were picked up, the dogs were in good health. Later, one of them had a litter of six *puppies*. The Russians gave one of the puppies to our President Kennedy."

Sheila held up her hands. "Okay, Gram, that's a good story," she said. "Now, what does all that have to do with Storm's name?"

"I was getting to that," Clara said. "One day, a year or two later, a stray Samoyed was found here in Gresham. The police took the dog to the Lawrences, because they kept Samoyeds. Imagine the family's surprise when they came home to find four white dogs instead of the usual three! Lots of people said the mystery Samoyed was a Russian space dog. Anyway, Storm is descended from her."

"Was she really a space dog?" Sheila asked, her eyes wide.

"I'm not saying she was," Clara said, laughing. "I just know that Storm loves to watch the space launches on television."

"Gram, you're too much," Sheila said. "Just for that, I'm going to study up on Samoyeds. As soon as I know all about them, I'll come back and tell you the real story."

A DOG FOR THE ICE AND SNOW

In the 1700s, an explorer gave the Samoyed its own species name, *Canis sibiricus*. That's Latin for "dog of Siberia." The name refers to the breed's origins in that northern Asian land. Modern scientists, however, classify the Samoyed in a different way. They say all dogs are meat-eating mammals of the scientific order *Carnivora*. Along with their closest cousins, the wolves, foxes, and jackals, dogs are part of the family *Canidae*. Every domestic dog, no matter where it comes from, belongs to the species *Canis familiaris*.

The Samoyed's everyday name comes from the Samoyedes, the Siberian tribe that developed the breed. These hardy people, with their black hair and dark skins, are related to the Inuits, the Eskimos of North America. Two centuries ago, the Samoyedes lived according to ancient traditions. Some were *nomads* who survived by hunting and fishing. Others herded reindeer for a living. Each group used its own dogs to pull sleds and guard its camps from hungry wolves.

The Samoyedes called their dogs "bjelkiers"

The Samoyeds get their name from the Samoyedes, a Siberian tribe that developed the breed.

— "white dogs that *breed* white." The Samoyeds had been raising their fine white dogs for at least 3,000 years. This makes the Samoyed one of the world's oldest breeds. By contrast, the reindeer herders bred working dogs that were mostly black-and-white or brown-and-white. On cold nights, both groups kept warm by sleeping with their dogs. When the temperature dropped very low, the Samoyedes called it a "two-dog night."

Stories of the Samoyedes and their beautiful dogs reached Europe in the 1800s. Explorers who were trying to reach the North and South poles bought Samoyeds to pull their sleds. Thanks to the dogs, the men were able to survive the hardships of exploring the poles. Some explorers tried to use horses to pull their sleds, but the animals died quickly in the bitter cold.

In 1889, an English traveler named Ernest Kilburn-Scott bought a brown Samoyed puppy from some Siberian natives. When he took Sabarka back to England, the dog was a great success. People fell in love with the Samoyed's furry good looks and sled-dog strength. In 1896, a cream-colored female named Whitey Pechora was imported to serve as Sabarka's mate. Even though Sabarka was brown, Whitey's puppies had white coats. More Samoyeds were imported. The breed grew in popularity. The names of these early dogs appear in the *pedigrees* of many Samoyeds today.

A Belgian countess brought the first four Samoyeds to the United States in 1906. One of them was a Russian champion named Moustan. Moustan was the first Samoyed registered by the American Kennel Club, AKC. A year later, one of Moustan's puppies became the first American champion. More dogs were

The first Samoyeds were brought to the United States in 1906.

imported. Owners worked hard to improve the breed. The country's long love affair with the sled dog from Siberia had begun.

EXPLORING THE POLES

By the 1890s, only two major parts of the world had not been explored. No one had yet set foot on either the North Pole or the South Pole.

The dangers of exploring the poles didn't stop a Norwegian named Fridtjof Nansen. Nansen believed he could make it to the North Pole with the help of several teams of Samoyeds. In 1895, he and a friend headed north from Greenland with 28 sled dogs. These were the best of the 40 dogs Nansen had purchased in Siberia.

Nansen admired the Samoyeds, but he treated them brutally. Right from the start, Nansen knew he couldn't carry enough dog food for the entire trip. In order to feed their teams, the explorers killed the weaker dogs and fed them to the stronger ones. The plan almost worked. The two men came very close

12

to the North Pole before they had to turn back. By then, only the two *lead dogs* were alive. When they reached open water, Nansen was afraid to take the dogs in the kayaks. He killed them, too.

In 1899, another Norwegian used Samoyeds to try to reach the South Pole. Carsten Borchgrevnik made a brave attempt, but he didn't succeed. Five years later, Borchgrevnik led another group across Antarctica, but failed again. This large expedition used over 100 Samoyeds to pull its sleds. Two of the dogs survived and were later taken to England. These dogs, Antarctic Buck and Trip, show up in the pedigrees of many modern Samoyeds.

A third Norwegian, Roald Amundsen, finally reached the South Pole in 1911. Amundsen bought 97 sled dogs. He picked 52 for his dash to the pole. The dog teams pulled four sleds, each loaded with supplies and a driver. A Samoyed lead dog was the first member of the expedition to cross the pole itself. The round-trip took 99 days and covered 1,800 miles. Because Amundsen followed Nansen's example, only 12 dogs were left at the end of the journey.

The explorers may have used their dogs cruelly, but they also admired them. Nansen reported his Samoyeds were loyal and friendly. At night, they would crowd around the men, begging to be petted. They also had great endurance. These dogs could cover almost 20 miles a day. At night, the dogs dug down into the snow and slept soundly. Only when someone tried *docking* a team's tails did the animals suffer from the cold. Without tails to curl around their muzzles at night, the dogs died of pneumonia.

In today's world, the Samoyed is more often a family pet than a sled dog. Every year, though, people in snowy regions of the world hitch up their dog teams to race cross-country.

Samoyeds are beautiful dogs that make excellent family pets.

The most beautiful teams are those that feature white dogs from Siberia. As they did for Nansen and Amundsen, the Samoyeds work hard for their drivers.

A CLOSE-UP OF THE SAMOYED

The Samoyed is a living picture of everything a fine dog should be. It is a beautiful, alert, and powerful dog. The heavy white coat tells you at once that the breed was created to work in ice and snow.

Samoyeds are medium-size dogs. The males stand about 22 inches at the *withers* (the top of a dog's shoulder). Females average two inches less. From chest to rump, the Samoyed is slightly longer than it is tall. A typical adult male weighs 52 pounds. The heavy coat makes the dog look larger than it really is. The long, coarse outer coat glistens with a silver sheen. The woolly undercoat is short and soft, perfect for weaving into a scarf or coat. Although most Samoyeds are pure white, a few are cream or biscuit colored.

The Samoyed carries its head upright on a strong, arched neck. The dark, almond-shaped eyes are deep-set in the skull and are circled by a thin rim of black fur. The head is broad and wedge shaped. The muzzle is of medium length, leading back to a well-defined *stop* (the rise between the dog's eyes). A Samoyed's furry ears are set high on its head. Shaped like rounded triangles, they stand proudly erect. The nose and lips are black, and the lips turn up at the corners. This gives many owners the feeling that their Samoyeds are grinning at them.

The Samoyed's body suggests power and pride. A great ruff of fur cloaks the shoulders and broad chest. The forelegs are straight. The strong hindquarters spread out slightly to give good balance. To complete the picture, the Samoyed carries its long, furry tail in a graceful, forward curl.

A Samoyed cuts its 28 baby teeth at three weeks. The 42 permanent adult teeth replace the baby teeth at four months. The dog's history as a *carnivore* can be read in these adult teeth. In its upper jaw, the Samoyed has 6 incisors (for cutting), 2 canines (for holding and tearing), and 12 molars and premolars (for slicing and crushing). The lower jaw has the same number of incisors and canines, but adds 2 extra molars. The canines have very deep roots, which increase their strength. Samo-

A Samoyed's furry body ends in a gracefully curved tail.

yeds that are fed soft foods often develop cavities and gum disease.

The Samoyed's history as a sled dog shows in its strength and endurance. A trained sled dog can pull up to 100 pounds. When moving at a normal trot, the left-front and right-rear feet move together. Then the right-front and left-rear feet swing forward. In the gallop, the front legs and the rear legs work as pairs. As the Samoyed springs forward, all four feet may be off the ground at the same time. The Samoyed never "grins" more happily than when it is pulling a sled through fresh snow.

A DOG'S-EYE VIEW OF THE WORLD

Can dogs think and solve problems? Most scientists say their brains are too small. After all, an adult Samoyed's brain only weighs about 3.5 ounces. By contrast, an average human brain weighs in at three pounds.

Lloyd Van Sickle is one man who doesn't believe the scientists. Some years ago, Van Sickle was carrying mail from Ashton, Idaho, to the West Yellowstone Ranger Station. In the winter, with roads closed, he covered the 64 miles by dog sled. On one trip, he ran into a blizzard. With eight feet of snow on the ground, he couldn't find the road. Not knowing what else to do, Van Sickle told his lead dog, "Go home!" Rex took off through the forest. The route was new to Van Sickle, but it led back to Ashton and safety.

How did the Samoyed solve the problem? Van Sickle figured it out a week later. Rex's keen ears had caught the humming sounds made by phone lines strung through the snow-covered trees. The dog knew the sounds meant "home," and he followed them there!

Whether Samoyeds can think or not, they see the world differently than do humans. For one thing, dogs are color-blind. They don't see well beyond 100 feet. Their close vision is poor. Perhaps that's why dogs can mistake a stranger's friendly gesture for a threat. Dogs see moving objects better than those standing still. If their noses don't detect a nearby skunk, they probably won't see it until the skunk moves. On the plus side, Samoyeds have a wider angle of vision than do humans. The dogs also have better night vision.

At birth, a puppy is blind and deaf. The eyes open at ten to fourteen days. The ears "open"

A Samoyed puppy is eager to play with its malamute friend.

about the same time. At that point, the puppy begins to learn the meanings of sounds. The dog's "sound world" extends well beyond what humans hear. Dogs hear higher tones and detect fainter sounds. Quick movements of its ears help a Samoyed locate the source of any sound. The use of a "silent" dog whistle proves that dogs hear sounds humans can't hear. The whistle produces sound at 30,000 cycles a second. Samoyeds respond at once. The person blowing the whistle hears nothing at all.

Of all the Samoyed's senses, its sense of smell is the strongest. Its nose contains many more nerve endings than the human nose does. Its brain is better at analyzing the air molecules that pass over these nerves. Tests show a dog can detect one drop of vinegar in 10,000 gallons. You may like the smell of roses, but a Samoyed prefers odors like sweat, blood, urine, and decaying meat. Chemical odors and the smell of smoke are unpleasant to a dog.

A Samoyed can track its owner down a busy city street or through a thick woods. Each person's scent is as individual as a fingerprint to the sharp nose of a dog.

THE SAMOYED'S SPIRITED PERSONALITY

Samoyed owners think their dogs have the best personalities in the dog world. As one woman writes: "Our Samoyeds will be your companions. They'd give you the coats off their backs if they could. All the while, they'll never allow life to become dull."

Some people say the Samoyed is the same as a husky. The Samoyed is related to the husky, but it's not the same dog. The word "husky" can be traced back to the Inuits. Inuit dogs became known as huskies. People who don't know any better call all sled dogs by that name. To the well informed, the name husky refers only to the smaller, darker-colored Siberian husky.

A Samoyed often selects one person as its "lead dog." This pattern began long ago when Samoyeds had to obey their master's whip and follow the team's lead dog. Despite this tendency, the Samoyed usually likes everyone in its family. As a *guard dog*, the Samoyed protects people better than property. A breeder warns new owners, "Once burglars are in the house, your Samoyed is likely to show them where you keep the silver. But if they threaten you, the dog will tear them apart."

Samoyed owners say it's easy to live with their dogs. Samoyeds like children. The dogs accept a lot of teasing and mauling. They're not so big as to knock down a toddler, but they're solid enough to endure rough handling. Around the house, they're graceful enough to avoid knocking over lamps and tables. That doesn't mean they won't try to share your easy chair! If you don't want a 50-pound lapdog, let your Samoyed know the facts of life early in its training.

Male and female Samoyeds have different personalities. The easygoing females seem proud to have their puppies handled by visitors. That's a good thing, because Samoyed puppies are like playful, fluffy snowballs. No one can resist them. The adult males, however, sometimes fight other Samoyed males. That habit goes back to a time when every male fought for leadership of the sled team. Male Samoyeds must be specially trained to ignore other males at dog shows.

Samoyeds aren't perfect. They're great chewers and diggers. A young dog will chew chair legs, shoes, and rugs. You'll have to keep a close eye on the dog until it can be trusted. As for digging, Samoyeds have been burrowing in the snow for thousands of years. When an Arctic storm strikes, they dig a hole, curl their tails over their noses, and wait out the storm. The habit is almost impossible to break. It's best to give the dog a place where it's allowed to dig. If this isn't possible, you may have to confine your Samoyed to a concrete run.

The breed adjusts to almost any type of life. If you're active, the Samoyed is ready to work or play. If you'd rather doze by the fire, the dog will keep you company. Most of all, Samoyeds want to please. They perform well in obedience training and in the show ring. When they do good work, they want to be praised. If a Samoyed is scolded without knowing why, it may sulk and refuse to work. That sounds almost human, doesn't it?

CHOOSING A SAMOYED PUPPY

"Dad, look at my report card," Chuck called. "You said if I brought up my grades, I could have a Samoyed puppy."

Ken Lando studied the report card. A pleased smile lit up his face. "That's a great improvement!" he said. "Now, how do you plan to find this puppy of yours?"

The question took Chuck by surprise. "I'll go to the pet store in the mall," he said at last.

Mr. Lando shook his head. "Pet stores stock only the best-selling breeds," he said. "When I checked, thirty-one other dogs were more pop-

When buying a Samoyed puppy, take a close look at its parents. The parents will show you how a puppy will look when it is an adult.

ular than Samoyeds. We'd better go to a breeder."

Chuck thought about that. "Where can we find one?" he asked.

"I talked to Dr. Clarke at the animal hospital," Mr. Lando said. "She gave me the name of a good kennel. Also, she says buying from a breeder will give you more puppies to choose from."

"That's what the book said!" Chuck broke

in. "Looking at a *purebred* puppy's parents gives you a picture of how it will look and behave when it's an adult. Also, the breeder can give us the puppy's papers so we can register our dog. That way we can show the dog or sell purebred puppies later on."

"I can't argue with that," Mr. Lando said. "The next thing is, do you want a male or a female Samoyed?"

"If I was starting a sled-dog team, I'd need a male to lead it," Chuck answered. "Females, though, are better house dogs. Besides, if I have a female, I can raise my own sled dogs."

"Good idea!" his father said, laughing. "Now, let's go see some puppies."

Helen Spencer was waiting for them at Sunburst Kennels. She took them out to a run where eight white Samoyed puppies were playing. "These rascals are nine weeks old. They're just the right age to leave their momma," she said.

Chuck picked up one of the dogs. The puppy squirmed and licked his face. "She's beautiful!" he shouted. "I'll take her!"

"Hold on a minute," Mr. Lando advised. "Look them all over."

As Chuck watched the puppies, he saw they weren't all alike. Some were bold and some

Healthy Samoyed puppies have bright eyes and clean, moist noses.

were shy. One big male seemed to be too aggressive.

Helen saw his confusion. "Do you want a *show dog* or a pet?" she asked. "That puppy over there is almost certain to be a champion. I'll have to ask $500 for her. The others are pet-quality dogs. They range from $250 to $400. A pet-quality Samoyed will have all the behaviors we love about the breed. It just won't win many points at a dog show."

"Are all these puppies healthy?" Ken wondered.

"I wouldn't sell a sick puppy," Helen assured him. "The *veterinarian* checked this *litter*. They've all had their puppy shots." She

If owners begin to train their Samoyeds when the dogs are puppies, they will have well-trained adult dogs.

pointed to the puppy Chuck was petting. "See, her eyes are bright and her nose is clean and moist. Her weight is good. Best of all, she likes people. I think she's a keeper."

Chuck nodded agreement. "Dad, let's take this one," he said.

Mr. Lando took out his checkbook. "Okay," he said, "but before we go, I want Helen to give you some advice on training that puppy. Your mom and I want her grades to be as good as yours."

TRAINING YOUR SAMOYED

How important is it to train your Samoyed? If you want to have a happy, well-behaved dog, training is everything. Dogs that aren't trained create problems for you and your neighbors.

Dog trainers know instinct drives a dog to compete for leadership of its "pack." You must let your Samoyed know you're the "top dog." This doesn't mean the dog has to fear you. The bonds you build with proper training are ties of love.

Training a Samoyed puppy begins soon after it's born. A breeder will start by turning the puppy onto its back. In that position, the puppy feels helpless. Then the breeder handles the puppy gently. This builds trust and lets the puppy get used to people. Little by little, the puppy is introduced to the outside world. Each step builds trust and confidence.

Here are some rules to follow when you train your Samoyed:

Start each command with the dog's name. Say, for example, "Chum, come!" in a firm, loud voice. That lets the dog know that it should get ready to obey. You can teach the "Come!" command by putting your dog on a long rope. When it wanders off, call it back. If it doesn't respond, yank on the rope. Repeat the process over and over until it gets it right.

Be consistent. Praise your dog each time it does something right. This lets it know it can earn more praise by doing the same thing again. Never overlook bad behavior. Laughing at bad behavior one time and scolding the next will only confuse your dog.

Hitting a dog won't solve the problem. Use your voice to correct your dog, not your hand. If your dog has soiled the carpet, tell it, "No! Bad dog!" Use a firm, loud voice. Smack the floor with a rolled-up newspaper. Then take the dog outside. Some owners shake very headstrong puppies by the loose skin at the back of the neck. This shaking doesn't hurt the puppies, and it gets their attention fast. But shaking an adult Samoyed in this way could injure the dog.

Always give a command in exactly the same way. Changing the wording of a command confuses a dog. Do not issue two or three commands at once. This will overwhelm even the brightest dog.

Practice makes perfect. Be prepared to practice each command over and over again. Your dog wants to learn, but it takes time to lock in new behavior.

You can apply these rules to any training situation. Use them when you *housebreak* your dog, for example. Also, it must learn the commands "Sit," "Stand," "Stay," and "Heel." A dog that heels properly is one that walks quietly at your left side. It won't go chasing after every cat, dog, and car that comes by. This command makes it possible to enjoy your daily walks. Remember, your Samoyed was bred to pull sleds. Without training, it may pull you wherever it wants to go!

CARING FOR YOUR SAMOYED

The scene is replayed every night in homes all over the country. Dad yells, "Who forgot to feed the dog?" The kids avoid his eyes until someone says, "Hobo is Mary's dog. She's the one who should feed him." Mary, of course, has gone to band practice.

Hobo, the Samoyed, looks at his family with sad, hungry eyes. His coat is matted and he has fleas. When he walks across the floor, his long toenails clatter on the hard surface. The family didn't know how much work Hobo would be when they bought him.

Proper care starts with a proper diet. After it's *weaned,* a puppy needs at least four meals a day of dry, packaged dog food. As the months go by, reduce the number of meals. A one-year-old dog is no longer a puppy. It needs only one meal a day. Along with regular feedings, always keep a bowl of fresh water where the dog can reach it.

Many breeders feed a dry dog food mixed with water or broth. During the winter, they give the dog extra fat. They feed their dogs suet, bacon fat, or corn oil. A little salt can be added in hot weather. This salt replaces the salt lost when the dog pants. Some owners prepare their own dog food. Here's a typical diet for a 40-pound Samoyed. Each day's feeding is made up of 24 ounces of cooked green beans, 9 ounces of lean beef, and 12 ounces of cottage cheese.

What you *don't* feed a Samoyed is just as important. Giving a dog table scraps and candy will give it a "sweet tooth." Dogs fed in this way develop cavities. They refuse their regular food and gain too much weight. Overweight dogs lose energy and die sooner. Also, never give fish or chicken bones to a dog. If these bones catch in the dog's throat, it may choke to death.

Next to its owner, a dog's best friend is its veterinarian. The vet keeps the dog's shot record up to date and spots problems before they become serious. If the dog has *worms,* for example, the vet can provide proper treatment. While you're there, you can ask the vet to tattoo your dog's AKC number on the inside of its hind leg. The tattoo will help you recover the dog if it's lost or stolen. Also, the vet can show you how to take your dog's temperature. A dog's normal body temperature ranges from 100.9 to 101.7 degrees Fahrenheit. A rise of two degrees is a signal the dog is ill.

Samoyeds are cold-weather dogs, but they adjust well to warm climates. In very hot weather, they like to cool off by putting their paws into a big pan of water. They also need a warm, dry doghouse that's large enough to stretch out in. You can use straw (or shredded newspapers) and an old blanket as bedding. Raise the floor of the doghouse off the ground to avoid cold and dampness.

Finally, Samoyeds need plenty of exercise and contact with people. If a dog is confined during the day, take it out for a long, fast walk each evening. A three-mile walk will do both of you a world of good! Being around people helps the Samoyed stay at its alert, outgoing best. Add proper grooming to this care, and a Samoyed should live for 12 or 13 years.

HELPING YOUR SAMOYED LOOK ITS BEST

Someone once said the Samoyed looks like a "walking cloud." It isn't easy to keep a Samoyed looking that way! The coat shows every speck of dirt. Rain brings out a strong, wet dog smell.

Grooming a Samoyed is a constant struggle. In good weather, sprinkle the dog with talcum powder or corn starch. When you brush it out, the powder takes some of the dirt with it. There's also the problem of shedding. A Samoyed male sheds once a year, a female twice. Vigorous combing and brushing will reduce the snowfall of hair that ends up on your furniture. It also encourages the growth of new hair. One woman saved her Samoyed's hair until she had enough to weave an eight-by-ten-

With the proper care, most Samoyeds live for 12 to 13 years.

foot rug. The rug was beautiful—and it didn't show a single hair that was shed on it!

Sooner or later, a Samoyed will need a bath. It's best to bathe your Samoyed in a regular bathtub. Run the warm water deep enough to soak the dog's legs and stomach. These are usually the dirtiest places. Use a good dog shampoo. Work the suds down to the skin. Then pour water over the neck and back. Save the dog's head till last. Use a washcloth to keep soapy water out of its eyes and ears.

After two complete latherings, you're ready to rinse. Use fresh, clear water. Rinse the Samoyed at least three times. If you don't remove all of the shampoo, the fur will look dull and lifeless when it dries. A creme rinse helps remove tangles. All this time, of course, your Samoyed will be sliding merrily around the tub. It will shake itself and splash water in all directions. Wear old clothes and have a mop handy.

Finally, remove the Samoyed from the tub and place it on a table. If you take the dog outdoors, it will roll in the dirt and undo all of your labor. With large towels, squeeze out most of the water. Comb out any tangles while the coat is still wet. Now, use a hair dryer to blow warm air over the dog's entire body. Brush lightly as you move the dryer back and forth. Most dogs enjoy this gentle attention. Keep it up until the coat is perfectly dry. Then comb out that lovely cloud of hair.

Four final steps will finish the grooming. First, check the dog's toenails to see if they need trimming. If you can hear them clacking on bare floors, they're too long. At the same time, cut the excess hair between the pads. Second, swab the area around the eyes with a cream sold in pet stores. The fluid from watery or teary eyes can stain the white fur.

Third, the ears should be swabbed to remove dirt and earwax. Swirl the cotton-tipped swabs slowly and don't poke too deep. Finally, check the dog's teeth. If they're stained, clean them with baking soda and a toothbrush. Let the vet remove any tartar that's built up.

By now you've invested an hour or more in grooming your Samoyed. Stand back and enjoy the sight. Have you ever seen a more beautiful animal?

BREEDING AND RAISING PUPPIES

Samoyed breeders know their dogs will breed true. The puppies all turn out like tiny white balls of fur. That's why people who own purebred females don't want puppies to "just happen." They want to mate the female (called a *bitch*) to a good male (the *stud*).

You can mate your Samoyed bitch when she's at least one year old. She should be in good health. Have her checked by a vet and bring her shots up to date.

Picking a male is the next step. If you don't

Newborn Samoyed puppies weigh about ten ounces, but they grow quickly on a diet of their mother's milk.

have a male of your own, find an owner with a champion stud. You're looking for a male with style, that "touch of class" that attracts people to the Samoyed. The easiest way to pay the stud fee is to give the owner the "pick of the litter." That means the breeder chooses one puppy. Take your dog to the stud on the tenth day of her next *heat.* Ask for a second mating if the first doesn't result in puppies.

Your dog will carry her puppies for nine weeks. During that time, she will need extra protein and lots of gentle exercise. As the eighth week begins, prepare a large wooden box and line it with newspapers. This is the *whelping* box. If you let your dog get used to the box, she won't try to give birth in your closet.

You'll know the time is close when your female tries to dig a hole in her whelping box. Put the box in a quiet place. Having too many people around will make her nervous. Each puppy is born headfirst, covered in its birth sac. The female will free the puppy from the sac. Then she'll lick it to help it start breathing. Next, she'll bite through the *umbilical cord*. With those jobs done, she'll give the puppy a second licking to clean and warm it. The next puppy will arrive about 30 minutes later.

If your dog's litter is typical, she'll have five or six puppies. Samoyed puppies are quite small. An average newborn weighs only about ten ounces. After the puppies start nursing, give the mother lots of fluids. This will help to get her milk started. Dog's milk has over three times the fat content of cow's milk. It's no wonder the puppies grow quickly! Their mother's milk will also help the puppies fight off disease.

Ask the vet to come by when the puppies

are a few days old. They need a checkup, and it's a good time to remove their *dewclaws*. These are the useless claws that grow on the front and hind legs of some dogs. By the time the puppies' eyes open, each newborn will have fluffy puppy fur. You'll laugh to see them trying to walk on wobbly legs. At four weeks, the mother will begin weaning her puppies. You can start feeding them a puppy diet of pablum and small bits of hamburger.

At eight weeks, the puppies will weigh about 14 pounds. That's a good time to find homes for them. Even if you sell them for a good price, you probably won't get rich. That doesn't matter. Playing with a litter of Samoyed puppies will give you a million dollars' worth of fun.

By eight weeks, Samoyed puppies weigh about 14 pounds and are ready for their new homes.

WHY DO SAMOYEDS BURY BONES?

After supper, Danny Ferris was drying the dishes while his sister washed. Outside, he and Kelsey could see the family's Samoyed chewing on a big beef bone. As they watched, Rascal picked up the bone and carried it into the garden.

"I hope he's not going to bury that bone," Danny said. "Mom will skin him alive if he digs up the tulip bed."

Kelsey smiled at her brother. "It looks like Rascal will start digging in about sixty seconds," she told him. "If you don't want him to get into trouble, you'd better move fast."

Danny ran out and caught Rascal just as he was starting to dig. "Give me the bone!" he ordered. Reluctantly, the big Samoyed opened his mouth. Danny led Rascal to his pen and gave him back the bone after he'd locked the gate. The Samoyed barked once, then lay down to gnaw on his bone.

Kelsey was behind him when Danny turned around. "Why does Rascal bury his bones?" he wondered aloud. "Did your college biology class teach you anything about dog behavior?"

"I learned enough to answer that question," Kelsey said, laughing. "It's all a matter of instincts left over from long ago. You know, of course, that dogs are descended from wolves."

"So, do wolves bury their bones?" Danny asked.

"It depends," Kelsey answered. "If a wolf kills a rabbit or any other small animal, it eats every scrap. It's different when a wolf pack brings down a moose. A wolf can eat up to twenty pounds of meat in a meal, but five or six wolves can't finish a big moose. If you were a wolf, what would you do next?"

Danny tried to think like a wolf. "If I leave the meat lying around, the vultures will eat it," he said. "So, I'd better hide it." He snapped his fingers. "I know, I'll drag it back to my den, where I can keep an eye on it."

"Wrong!" Kelsey said. "Leaving meat in the den creates two problems. First, other wolves might steal it. Second, flies will lay their eggs on the meat and it will soon be full of maggots. Wolves have strong stomachs, but they won't eat rotten meat unless they're starving."

"Okay, I'll have to bury my leftover moose leg," Danny decided. "That will keep the flies away. Still, the meat will be covered with dirt when I dig it up again."

"Look at Rascal," Kelsey said. "The dirt doesn't bother him. A wolf digs up its meat within a day or two, shakes it a few times, and gulps it down."

Danny tried to apply the lesson to his own dog. "Rascal was already full when I gave him the bone," he said. "So, he tried to save it for later. If that's true, why doesn't he try to save his regular dog food?"

"I think dogs see bones as something worth saving," Kelsey replied. "Burying dry dog food probably seems like a waste of time."

"Well, at least I know Rascal is getting enough to eat," Danny said. "If he was really hungry, he'd never try to bury a good bone like that one."

SAMOYEDS ARE NATURAL SLED DOGS

It was the winter of 1925. Nome, Alaska, had been hit by an epidemic of diphtheria, a deadly illness. The lifesaving medicine was in

Nenana, 675 miles away. The airport and rail-road were closed. Only dog sleds could get through.

The Great Serum Run was a relay race against death. The snow was waist deep, and ice formed jagged ridges along the route. Mile after long mile, the teams carried their precious cargo toward Nome. The drivers often lost their way, but the sled dogs brought them through. Five and a half days later, Gunnar Kasson drove the last relay leg into Nome. Kasson's dogs were running on bloody feet, and the driver was half frozen. He gave much of the credit to Balto, his great lead dog.

Today, Alaska remembers that historic run in a yearly dog-team race called the Iditarod. The race is named for the old Iditarod Trail. The race covers 1,049 miles. The drivers (known as "mushers") come from Alaska, Canada, the "lower 48" states, and Europe. Each musher trains and drives a team of 15 to 18 dogs. The rules state the teams must finish with at least seven dogs. This allows mushers to leave sick or lame dogs at checkpoints along the way. The 1988 winner completed the race in a record 11 days.

Samoyeds are more often seen in shorter races. Drivers look for dogs with long legs and light bones. Training begins when puppies are two months old. A trainer may tie several puppies behind their mother to teach them to pull together. More serious training starts when a puppy is harnessed to a small log. Watching the puppy pull the log gives the owner a good idea of the dog's spirit. Next, the Samoyed moves on to pulling a small sled. In warmer climates, a three-wheeled cart can be used.

Soon, two or more dogs can be harnessed together as a team. Training runs take them out on the local trails. The dogs must learn to pull together and keep their minds on the job. The driver controls the team with a few simple commands. When the dogs perform well, praise *reinforces* the good behavior. At two years old, a dog can cover 15 miles at a good speed. As training continues, the team picks its own lead dog.

A team is only as good as its leader. In the old days, the lead dog won its job by defeating the other dogs. After the fight, the rest of the team sometimes ate the final loser. It's no surprise that in Russian, the word "Samoyed" has come to mean "cannibal." As soon as a lead dog showed any weakness, it had to be replaced. That was the only way to save its life.

Getting started in racing isn't easy. You'll

need at least three eager-to-work Samoyeds and a light sled. To hook up the dogs, you'll need a leather harness, lines, and collars. After you've trained your dogs, you can enter your first race.

Now it's time. The starter waves a flag. You step onto the runners and shout the traditional starting command. At your call of "Mush!" your team is off and running.

GLOSSARY/INDEX

Bitch 37—An adult female dog.

Breed 9, 37—To mate a quality bitch to a stud.

Carnivore 8, 16—A meat-eating animal.

Dewclaws 40—Extra, useless claws that grow on the insides of a dog's legs. These are removed by a vet at birth.

Docking 14—Shortening a dog's tail by cutting it off at the first or second joint.

Grooming 5, 34, 36, 37—Bathing and brushing a dog to keep its coat clean and smooth.

Guard Dog 22—A dog that's been trained to protect people and property.

Heat 38—The time when a bitch is ready to mate.

Housebreak 31—To train a puppy so it doesn't relieve itself inside the house.

Lead Dogs 13, 19, 22, 44, 45—The "boss" dogs of sled-dog teams.

Litter 27, 38—A family of puppies born at a single whelping.

Nomads 8—A group of people who move about from place to place in search of food, water, and grazing land.

Pedigrees 10, 13—Charts that list dogs' ancestors.

Although Samoyeds are cold-weather dogs, they adjust well to warmer climates.

GLOSSARY/INDEX

Puppies 7, 10, 19, 20, 23, 24, 25, 26, 27, 28, 29, 30, 32, 37, 38, 39, 40, 44, 45—Dogs under one year of age.

Purebred 25, 26, 37—A dog whose ancestors are all of the same breed.

Reinforces 45—Gives a dog a reward when it obeys a command.

Show Dog 27—A dog that meets the highest standards of its breed.

Stop 16—The area between a dog's eyes.

Stud 37, 38—A purebred male used for breeding.

Umbilical Cord 39—The hollow tube that carries nutrients to the puppy while it's inside the mother's body.

Veterinarian 27, 33, 37, 39—A doctor who is trained to take care of animals.

Weaned 32, 40—When a puppy stops nursing from its mother.

Whelping 39—The birth of a litter of puppies.

Withers 15—The dog's shoulder, the point where its neck joins the body. A dog's height is measured at the withers.

Worms 33—Dangerous parasites that live in a dog's intestines.